Laura Barnes
Lottie Bluewater
Erin Craine
Olivia Furness
Lola Garlick
Eva Gaynor-Smith
Eleanor Hall
Mollie Hurrell
Martha Jamieson
Ellie Sammer
Emily Louise Todd
Angelica Willis

**THEATRE
IN THE
ROUGH**

Published by Theatre in the Rough in 2024
theatreintherough.com
Registered Charity No. 1133246
ISBN: 978-1-7393825-5-1

Director
Jessica Meade

Jessica is a director based in the North West. She received attachment training with the Liverpool Everyman and Playhouse, and has also been a member of Open Exchange, The Manchester Royal Exchange's director development scheme. She opened the 2022 autumn season for the Liverpool Everyman Theatre with *A Billion Times I Love You* by Patrick Maguire. Jessica was recently awarded The Buzz Goodbody Director's Award 2023 by The Royal Theatrical Trust for *TOUCH*, which was selected to feature at the National Student Drama Festival.

Designer
Joseph Rynhart

Joseph works with charitable and creative organisations to bring cultural programmes to life through design. Often this is through print, digital work, or animation; and sometimes through exploring uncharted territories of wood, metal, and paint. Previous clients include English Heritage, Lincoln Arts Centre, and the British Olympic Association. Previous commissions include work for Curious Minds, The Financial Times, and the People's History Museum.

Artistic Director, Theatre in the Rough
Chris Fittock

Chris founded Theatre in the Rough in 2009. He is also a playwright and dramaturg. He has co-created five nationally touring productions with Tmesis Theatre, and his work has appeared across the UK, and in New York and San Francisco. He has also written for the BBC and Channel 4. He is published by Nick Hern.

SKYGLOW was first performed at Sudley Walled Garden, Liverpool, 16–18 August, 2024.

Sudley Walled Garden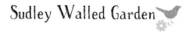

Thanks

We are grateful to Lucy Dossor and Growing Sudley CIC for supporting this project, and providing us with the most glorious plot of earth to perform in. If you have theatre and a garden, you have everything.

growingsudley.com

We are also grateful to Dr Mark Norris from the Jeremiah Horrocks Institute (UCLan), and Professor Tim Smyth from Plymouth Marine Laboratory, who encouraged deep thinking and wide imaginings in our writers.

Funders

SKYGLOW is made possible thanks to funding awarded by Postcode Neighbourhood Trust and raised by players of People's Postcode Lottery; The PH Holt Foundation; The Granada Foundation; The Sylvia Waddilove Foundation; and The Unity Theatre Trust.

INTRODUCTION

Lands in my bedroom.
I get out of bed and grab it.
Get something that floats and
Get it back into the sky.
Because I want stars to shine
For everyone.

How can you see stars when they're in space?

Cracks.
Sad.
Can you try?

What can we do to help you shine brighter?
Bonfire Night: Sparks look like stars.
Can you shine a bit brighter?
Happy.
Excited.
I want people to get home.
Not lost.
Turn all the lights off.

— by Emily Louise Todd

Emily's poem captures the spirit of this anthology of plays about the dying of the light. It tells us that starlight is precious because it's both present and absent; and it gently asks us to consider how we'd navigate without it – disarrayed and alone in vast, unlit space.

The truth is, the skies are dying and the constellations are in crisis. A child born beneath tonight's stars will see less than half of them by the time they're eighteen. This is due to 'skyglow' – the haze of artificial light pollution dimming the brilliance of the cosmos. The problem is also worsening with the rapid increase of low-orbit satellites. Artificial mega-constellations are increasing exponentially. While the first half-century of space exploration saw 1,000 such bodies launched, there may well be 100,000 circling above our heads by 2030. We risk, indeed, unwittingly trapping ourselves on Earth, unable to navigate through the orbiting space debris.

This celestial crisis threatens millennia of navigation, myth-making, and indigenous traditions. But the impact of skyglow extends beyond the stars. By disrupting the natural transition from sunlight to starlight, it interferes with the behaviour, physiology and delicate balance of many of Earth's species – over half of which are nocturnal.

SKYGLOW aims to illuminate these startling effects of light pollution on both nature and culture. It's an invitation to witness our vanishing night sky and confront humanity's cosmic impact on the universe.

As the boundary between earth and sky blurs, a group of eco-conscious writers have crafted stories spanning from soil to stardust. Their words, created in collaboration with astronomers and ecologists, paint a vivid picture of the changing universe and our place within it.

We want people to get home. Not lost. So, turn all the lights off . . . and, perhaps, we can shine a little brighter.

CHRIS FITTOCK
Artistic Director, Theatre in the Rough

SKYGLOW

The Luminous

By Laura Barnes

MOTH. Tonight, the air is heavy,

Blowing the floral scent of jasmine and vanilla across the
cool cobbled street,

Dew drops hang from the branches of trees and fall into
the neat fridges of cut grass below,

Ants march across the landscape of scattered puddles, a
jigsaw of twigs hide in the soil, and the electricity wires
hum a nighttime melody,

I rub my eyes, it's been a restless day of hot slumber,

Where sleep was hindered by awkward contortions and
noisy neighbours, and I can't wait to stretch out and
breathe,

I unstick myself from brick, shake off the clinging
cobwebs and drift upwards to freedom,

My powdery fluttering makes me rise and glide and fall
and soar, admiring the length and depth of my shadow
below and the grace of Orion in the sky above

. . .

All at once,

I break into a sprint, hurling faster and faster, flapping
my sides frantically,

I feel the breeze beneath my wings, the taste of iron in my
mouth, and the surge of lightning through my body,

I must go faster, I must climb higher . . . but to where?
And what from? I have no idea,

And I'm panicking and I'm darting around and all I can
see is the dazzle of a light in the distance above me,

A radiant orb,

A ghostly pearl,

A rare jewel,

Enticing me to its gleaming lair,

It grows bigger and brighter and wider until,

My body fumbles against its hot surface, scorching my wings,

I bounce backwards,

Shocked and stunned at the hellish back hole it's branded,

Confused and dazed, I turn to escape but my eyes are entranced by the glow, and the invisible strings it's tied around me make me a shadow puppet of its bright command

. . .

As I twist around,

I meet a melting embrace of fellow creatures, all circling the same blazing glow,

My senses are shattered, my vision is blurred,

I cannot make out wing from antennae from furry body to waxy leg,

A phantom frenzy of ravers, sipping the light in tiny red plastic cups,

A robotic response to coming of age,

Across the curved dancefloor,

It's a humdrum of swaying and spinning, of high kicks, body rolls and violent swivels,

Of sharp shapes and dodging divers and flapping and
tapping and flitting and zooming and whirling,

Like dirty laundry spinning against the metal machine,
we drunkenly swim together, fighting for air in the
rapids,

Somehow, it feels that there is a comradery in this shared
dizziness,

Some fly higher, some quicker, some beat their wings
harder than others, but we all beat together in a
rhythmical revolt,

A symposium of silent screams where our tongues are
too tied for a sing-along,

Relentless, restless, we keep going, and we endure,
hoping that this ride, this merry-go-round of horrors
might end soon,

But however much we hope, we all know,

That this is a nightly festival,

A sold-out, regular revival,

Where tired souls will return tomorrow, to search for the
spotlight,

And labour in its rays

. . .

In the chaos, I catch the glimpse of a haggard face,

A smudge of grey whirling past me in the haze,

A smear in my periphery,

His strained voice reverberates around,

'Oh, it didn't used to be like this — back in my day the night was calm,

there were different shapes in the sky, and I flew straight across the cobbles —

Oh, how everything's changed, the whole world's gone mad.'

Could this be a cloudy memory?

A sign of lunacy?

Or the words of a scatter-brained fool?

And I giggle to myself at the dizzy thought,

How could it be different before?

. . .

Sometimes a new face will refresh the memory, pushing towards the crowded inner circle,

Forcing an unlucky guest to tumble out of the loop,

Just because I don't see the fall, does not mean I don't hear the splatter on the concrete or the scratch of a bird's talon on the tarmac, to lap up the mess,

And each time it happens, I am grateful for the light that holds my gaze, shielding me from the contents of that rubbery surface,

And each time, I think of myself as a white speckled fairy,

A graceful air acrobat pointing my toes and nimbly leaping past the others,

It's comforting to have such a radiance shining over me, it is our Saviour and protector, our ever-present God watching the chaos below

. . .

And as I admire it, she winks at me and releases me from her trance,

I zigzag downwards at such a pace that I almost hurdle deep down into the earth, almost crashing into the mantle and it's burning core,

But something soft catches me, it's warm and smells of lavender, and it soothes my aching body and pounding head,

Very slowly, I unweave the material stitch by stitch, carefully nibbling each thread until there is space to nestle in and collapse inside,

My body is still, and I am alone to rest once more,

The sky undulates above me, the fleet of constellations sail slowly ahead, and I wonder . . .

for how long can we outrun the light?

I whisper: take me to the darkness to chew through the layers of the deep blue fabric where we will drink the cool water and feast amongst the stars,

Because in the dark we are beautiful, delicate specks of the universe,

but when the sunlight burns, we become drab dust at dawn.

The End.

Punch Me in the Head, I Want to See Stars!

By Lottie Bluewater

ZO. Punch me in the head, I want to see stars!

Smack me right across the skull with a great big frying pan

Drop apples on my head, Isaac Newton-style

Bonk my cranium as hard as you can

Thwack, knock, smack and clobber

So that I can see those shimmering little beads of light

Pearls of the sky

Bonk me with enough force and I'd open my eyes to an explosion of rhinestones!

Scattered across the silky blue-black

Pulling out their best dance routine for me

Carefully choreographed over billions of years to entice me in.

I would finally understand an astronomer's fascination, they live up there

Head in the clouds

They couldn't help it, they got drawn in

And now they spend their lives amongst the stars

And I don't blame them for that

I mean, imagine,

Being surrounded by those glowing beacons with their little beams

So radiant.

And dancing so seductively, I want to join them too!

I'd hop on one of the shooting ones

And go zooming across the galaxy

A portal of gases and glows

Do you think it smells?

I once read about the smell of a comet

The Rosetta spacecraft came across comet 67P/Churyumov-Gerasimenko, and found some prettty stinky molecules in its gassy halo

They reckon it could be quite the cocktail,

Ammonia's urine-like scent, mixed up with eggy hydrogen sulphide and pickled formaldehyde,

To sweeten it up — hydrogen cyanide's almondy aroma and sweet carbon disulfide.

Although I'm not sure that would be enough to mask the rest of the stink.

That wouldn't matter so much I guess,

It'd be pretty cool to see (or smell) a comet up close on my shooting star ride!

While I'm up there, I'd see if the constellations look different.

My friend and I used to go stargazing at Scout camps,

We'd sneak out of our tent when the leaders were asleep and sit by the burnt-out fire,

Perhaps a couple of glowing embers would linger,

But not enough to distract from the twinkling above us.

We made a map of what we saw, we became explorers
navigating our own way through the night sky.

Just two peas in a pod, two interstellar travellers,

With our joint mission to chart the night.

I still have my star map stuck on my wall — I wonder if
he does too . . .

So of course I can spot the Big Dipper, the Little Dipper,
the North Star,

Sometimes Cygnus or Lyra on a really clear night.

And I'm all too familiar with Orion's belt,

But I'd love to get to know the man behind the girdle!

I'd take a visit to see the archer, the Sagittarius
constellation

Down in the southern celestial hemisphere.

That's my star sign, so I should probably take a look.

Anyway, so imagine you've thwacked me across the head

And I've woken up find to a sparkling expanse above me

And now I'm up there.

Me on my meteor, exploring the universe in a way that
no one has before

Yeah, I might be a little bit scared.

But this is what I asked for.

Right?

I want to see them,

I want to see stars.

I remember it being beautiful up there,

I remember from being a kid,

I remember thinking 'she's so elegant, the sky; her velvet drapes and the pearls and jewels that hang from all parts of her!'

How could we not worship her?

And I'm not religious but I must confess,

I like the idea of floating up into the ether when I pass from this world to the next.

But what a lonely experience that would be if no one's able to look up for me.

I hope my nan and my first cat, Brad, are okay up there, not too lonely,

I still look up for them,

And they've got each other, I guess.

But it won't be long before we have to strain our eyes when looking up into the skies,

A curtain is being drawn between us and the night.

From the ground where I stand, most stars are out of sight.

And it almost feels like there is no nighttime.

As a kid when I couldn't sleep,

My parents would take me on nighttime drives.

As I got a bit older, I still couldn't sleep

So I would lie awake, listening to the ruckus of the seagulls all through the night,

Opening my curtains to let in the moonlight.

The night before GCSE results day, I stayed awake till 3am,

Unintentionally, I just couldn't doze off.

So I sat in my garden, and the stars sat there with me.

In my late teens, I'd go for midnight wanders,

Sometimes with a (now) ex-boyfriend, sometimes by myself.

Not the safest, in hindsight, but I felt sheltered under the starlight.

When I went to uni, me and my flatmates, now my best friends,

Would stay awake all night long, playing countless rounds of Uno and getting a little gin-drunk.

We would open the windows of our fourth-floor flat,

Singing songs from our childhood.

Most notably *Rule the World* by Take That,

Serenading the stars above us.

We butchered it, of course.

A really fond memory of mine,

Spans the summer after I turned eighteen,

My friends and I would go out clubbing on the weekend,

And the weekdays to be fair.

We'd leave the club when it was still dark

And hop on the last bus together,

Gradually we'd say goodbye as one by one my friends got off at their respective stops.

Mine was the last one.

And when I arrived it was just getting light, 4am, almost ready for sunrise,

I'd unlock my front door, still giddy and silly with drink

And I would turn to salute the moon for escorting me home.

Then I'd look to Orion and give him a nod, as if to say, 'Thanks mate, thanks for seeing me back safe!'

And off to bed I went.

As you can probably tell, me and sleep have never got on well,

So the night has been a faithful friend.

We've spent a hell of a lot of time together,

And now we know each other well, I'd say.

But I've noticed her changing, dimming.

And sometimes, it feels like I don't know her very well at all any more.

Now, when I open my curtains to let in the moonlight,

My bleary eyes squint out to see the lights of the night:

Orange taxi beams zipping around, returning the intoxicated to their homes and to their beds,

The cold white of the multi-storey car park,

Flashing blue and red, with synchronised sirens,

A soft amber glow from a single flat in the otherwise dull, brutalist high-rise across the road, I watch the two new lovers talking through the night, intertwined in the gentle light of their own blushes and beams . . .

Helicopter searchlights.

Open signs, Closed signs.

An icy haze rising from the water, where boats and cruise ships are docked.

Petrol stations, kebab shops, and strobes escaping the clubs dotted across the city.

The lights of the night.

Not the stars, or the moon, but the blaze from the ground.

Can I see the sky please?

So once you've sent me into space with a bonk to the brain,

And I'm on my meteor, and I've seen Sagittarius and I've smelt a comet,

I'm up there with my memories,

All the parts of my life I experienced under starlight.

Up there with my friend, the night sky.

Can I see the sky please?

As the stars disappear to the naked eye,

I can't understand how you can just stand by,
unbothered.

Are you not frightened?

Do you not care?

That we're losing the night, because of human glare.

I'll grab a pan in a minute, or my fist might do,

Thwack you over the head, knock some sense into you.

I need to see stars forever, and I want you to too.

So go on then, punch me!

Punch me!

Or dim the lights, just a little

Well actually maybe a lot,

If you don't mind.

'Cos I'd rather not wake up with a huge lump on the side
of my head

And I'm sure you'd rather not punch me.

So just turn off the lights.

And that the hazy glow of the city will grow fainter and fainter and slowly vanish,

Neon signs, LED billboards, streetlamps,

All gone.

And I can wander freely under the cover of night.

I can cast my eyes upwards towards our galaxy, finally bright again.

When I was born,

My dad held me up to the hospital window, as my mum had her tummy sewn back up.

It was quarter past twelve in the morning,

My wrinkly little face, fresh into this world, looked out into the night,

My scrunched-up eyes took their first glance up into space

And I saw stars.

I didn't need a knuckle to the skull.

I saw my first stars on that mid-December morning,

And I have never stopped looking up.

So, if you won't punch me (that is kind of frowned upon I suppose),

Then I guess you should find some other way of ensuring the stars stick around.

Go on then —

I'm waiting.

The End.

Echo Chamber

By Erin Craine

30

SURVEYOR ONE. Diagnostic Report #21013 at oh-eight-hundred hours. This is Surveyor One, do you copy?

Waits. Listens, but doesn't expect anything. No one answers.

I thought not. Nothing to report. Over.

The same as usual. No one answers — and no one has answered for a very long time. SURVEYOR waits. This time will be different. It has to be.

This is Lunar Lander Surveyor One requesting contact — over.

No one answers.

You know, I thought this was funny at first, but it's starting to get kind of annoying now. I just want a transmission, an update, something. Don't be shy.

No one answers. SURVEYOR dares to wonder.

Maybe you're not awake yet. Maybe you're late for work. Maybe you're always late for work, and that's why we keep missing each other. Wouldn't that be funny? Wouldn't that be just like you?

There's almost a fondness there — a memory from a machine. It's not reciprocated.

I've taken pictures of the surface like you asked me to. Over 11,237 of them. I sent them down to you during Diagnostic Report #7, but I can send them again if you missed them that time. Or the time after that. Or the time after that.

They're beautiful, even with this old lens and the motion blur, but I suppose you knew that. Why else would you send me to take them? Why wouldn't you want a better look?

They're not a patch on the real thing, though. They don't properly capture the way the dust shines when I'm sandwiched between you and the Sun, glittering like all those little metal shavings on the lab floor, from where you've drilled out channels for bolts and rivets. They don't quite get the darkness either — when the Moon is at the furthest point of its orbit, and I'm staring out into space, not quite sure if there's something out there, staring back at me.

Sometimes I wonder if it'll never swing back round, but I wait a few moments, you always come back into view eventually. I always miss you. Do you miss me too?

SURVEYOR speaks aloud with a sense of familiarity — yet refuses to wonder if the only person listening is itself. No one answers, but SURVEYOR continues as if someone has.

I can take more if you like — they'd have some satellites floating about in them, but it's impossible to avoid them now. If you brought me back, I could be launched in a different direction, and take pictures of entirely new things — things you didn't even know existed. There's so much up here, you wouldn't believe it.

Beat.

Well, you'd probably believe it if you saw the pictures.

A touch of sarcasm — perhaps concealing bitterness. But SURVEYOR doesn't sit in it for long.

You know, it feels like just yesterday you shot me up into orbit, all enthusiastic and hazy with smoke. I was so used to being surrounded by people, talking and calculating and scribbling away, that I didn't even think about how quiet it would be up here.

I remember one of you had a moustache like a bristle brush — the one that left an oily handprint on the inside of my delta wing. It's about time that got cleaned up. Or maybe you can add another one to make it a pair? I'd be happy either way. I'd be happy to see a face, any face.

Or hear a voice.

Anything.

No one answers.

It's weird how quickly things can change, isn't it?

You all spend every second of every day of your lives revolving around this huge, burning ball of gas, but when you get into orbit, it's like you're the only thing up here. Like falling into nothingness, and being spat out somewhere that doesn't entirely exist yet.

I can still see you if I squint — if the angle is right, and the Sun isn't in the way, messing up the exposure. I can focus the lens just enough to see the little green blob you launched me from. It's gotten harder recently, new machines keep popping up into orbit like chicken pox, but every so often I can catch a glimpse. Can you see me too? Do you look up at the sky, and wonder if I'm above you?

SURVEYOR waits. No one answers.

Do you know you're getting brighter?

I know the sky is supposed to be brighter where people are, but if that's true, then people must be everywhere. How do you breathe? Where do they all go?

It's so bright now it shines off of you like a halo, just visible through the junk.

I've only been up here for 219 days, four hours, and sixteen minutes, but it's spreading so fast I can barely see the stars. I used to be able to tell where all the big cities were, just from the shapes of the lights — London like a spiderweb, California and New York on either side of America like brackets — but they've been growing like tumours into one big sparkling puddle — on and off and on again like clockwork when you all go to bed at nighttime. You must know. You must see it — the wildfires in the papers, the Gilbert Islands, the Ellice Islands, just washing away into dust. You must feel the heat, humid and thick in the summer, only for the snowstorms to bury you in the winter.

And while it's all falling apart, you're still going, even with everything starting to slide away into the ocean — a new cluster of lights, a new crop of buildings, a new satellite, a new hunk of metal left to rot in orbit, and not a single one of them can tell me what's going on. Everything I send gets ignored, and anything I pick up is scrambled into white noise nonsense. They're like nothing I've ever seen before, shiny and sleek — sitting there in their masses, dancing around each other, echoing into emptiness, waiting for *you* to do something.

They'll hit each other eventually, you know, and go plummeting straight back down to you in a million little shards, while the world keeps turning, and growing, and changing, and aging like nothing's wrong. Why is everything changing so quickly? It's only been seven months, but destruction on this scale would take a lifetime — *several* lifetimes. It doesn't make sense.

Don't you know?

Don't you care?

SURVEYOR waits.

Are you listening?

No one answers.

Maybe you can't hear me. Maybe my equipment broke, and you're trying to fix it, and you can't wait to see the pictures I've sent. Maybe you're still busy with the *big* project, making me a friend, or sending someone up to keep me company. Someone who can actually understand me, and doesn't just sit there, turning in orbit and gathering dust.

No one answers. SURVEYOR, for perhaps the first time, feels some way about it.

But I did what you asked me to. I fulfilled my purpose — I *surveyed*. The first American space probe to land on the Moon, or anything, for that matter. I can come home now. I'd like to come home. It's lonely. Even surrounded by a hundred million machines, I'll always be lonely.

I'm sure you're working on it. *Man on the Moon* — the Apollo rocket — it can't be that long now. They'll take me home with them, and then I can survey somewhere else. Get another handprint. Take more pictures. See more.

It'll take a while to get through all of the satellites, but you'll get here. I just need to be patient. I'm sure you're on your way. I'll be right here, waiting. I can't wait to see you all again.

Just a little bit longer. It'll be any minute now. Any minute now. Any minute now. Any minute.

SURVEYOR waits. No one answers.

The End.

Just What I Needed

By Lola Garlick

38

The present. The only light is from the stars above. Sitting in a field looking up is AVA. Suddenly she looks towards the audience.

AVA. I was meant to go on a date tonight.

The past. AVA pulls her phone out of her hoodie pocket. She looks at the time.

Shit. It's 6pm.

She is in her bedroom.

I'd shut my curtains earlier this afternoon so I could have a power nap without the disruption of the sun shining in my face as my alarm clock — but the problem with that was that I then had no alarm, and wake up in complete panic mode.

With blurred vision and pillow-imprinted marks on my face I open my curtains to see the sun setting behind the cathedral. A sight, that on any other day, I would take time to watch. But not today.

Prep time, and by that I mean showering, shaving, blow-drying, straightening, blushing, bronzing, pulling everything out of my wardrobe because, although I have enough clothes to own a shop, I can't find anything to wear.

It's 8pm by the time I finally find an outfit (all black of course, because to wear colour would deffo be pushing the boat out).

I then have to FaceTime my sister, my best friend and my mum for opinions on the fit. Simple protocol I suppose. That's when it started raining, which meant I had to find a jacket. That was hell. Leather jacket? No. Too much black. Looks cheap. Too long. Coat? No. Too chunky. Gonna be a nightmare to carry around. Oversized shirt. No.

Frustrated, fast thoughts.

Just gonna get soaked, then I'll be wet and cold, my mascara will run, and my hair will turn into a frizz ball. Coat it is.

It's 9pm. We're meeting at a cute wine bar, and it's only a short walk from me so I think I will be safe from a frizz-ball nightmare. I can't remember much of the walk there because I was consumed with all kinds of thoughts: Do I look okay? Maybe I should have worn my jacket instead?

I arrive and scan the bar, but I am fashionably early.

Wine bar. AVA walks to a table and sits down, facing the audience.

I find a table towards the back of the bar and sit facing the door. I scan the menu. I know we agreed to go to a wine bar, but I don't actually drink wine . . . I was too scared to say I'm not a wine drinker in case that was a red flag for him. I asked the waiter for a bottle of their most popular red and I take tiny sips in the hope that I won't really be able to taste it. That doesn't work. I pull a wincing face after every sip.

She looks at her watch.

I'm no longer fashionably early. He's ten minutes late. I message him saying 'I'm here :)', and he reads it almost straight away, so he must nearly be here. I look towards the door whenever someone enters, preparing myself for it to be him

She looks to her watch again.

Fifteen minutes. Twenty. I begin to worry.

I look at the bottle on the table practically full, and the empty glass opposite me. I look back to the door and feel a slight relief when I see someone who I think could be him. I give him a big smile and he waves. I wave back. He walks towards me. I stand up to greet him. He walks past me. To a table behind me. He greets a girl that must be his girlfriend: I know this because they share a kiss that is intimate and loving like the movies. I'm mortified.

I sit back down as quickly as I can, wishing the ground would open up and swallow me whole. I think it's safe to say I've been stood up. No one has noticed me sitting alone, I mean why would they? I scan the room full of couples holding hands across the table, staring into each other's eyes, completely besotted with the person sitting opposite them. I feel invisible. Forgotten.

I give the couple behind me the rest of the bottle. They both smile and thank me, and with that I grab my bag and leave as quickly as I can.

Once I'm outside I take a breath. One of those ones runners do when they finish their last mile.

I hear my name being called — it's my course mates. If it wasn't for the streetlamp I was standing under, they would have passed without noticing me. I told them earlier in the day I was going on a date so I wouldn't be able to join them at the pub. They cross the road and ask me how my date was (with slurred words). My social battery is running low so I tell them the situation in as little words as possible.

One of the girls, clearly having consumed too many glasses of wine, pulls me in for a hug and goes on a rant about how all boys are the same and that I'm better off without him.

She's probably right, especially after how shit he's just made me feel. I say I just want to go home to bed but they are practically dragging me down the road, so I didn't really have a choice.

It's 10.30pm.

We make our way through crowds of uni students mixed with hen parties and their inflatable husbands to be. Strobe lights lead the way through the hectic streets. I'm barged by multiple early peakers stumbling to the next bar, too consumed by the glow of their phone screens to look where they're going. I'm contemplating whether this was a good idea. I've fallen behind the group after being harassed by a drunk middle-aged man saying how pretty I was. That's the only compliment I've received all evening.

I make it to the bar. It's packed: bodies-pressing-against-one-another kind of packed. I push myself through the crowds to the bar where my course mates are doing shots — they've saved one for me so I quickly down it before following them into the sea of sweat, spilt drinks and random limbs flailing sporadically, glistening from the mirror ball's reflection. I dance to a couple of songs, but after having my foot trodden on multiple times and my sleeve drenched in someone's vodka lemonade, it was time to leave.

I try to get one of the girls' attention to tell her I was leaving, but she was too busy talking to a boy she had spotted from the bar, so I make a swift exit, convinced the group won't even realize I've left.

It's 11.30pm.

I'm yet again manoeuvring through the rush hour of the night: flashes from phones as girls pose for Instagram, bouncers flinging club doors open, letting out bright white strobes and kicking out underage kids, queues flowing out of chicken shops as people make a pit stop on their walk home, and I'm alone again. I think that's why I don't often go 'out out'. I'd much prefer to have a few ciders in a beer garden and get an early night — but when I'm surrounded by people who crave the feeling that comes with dancing with strangers at 3am, my preferences are overlooked.

I reach the mammoth hill that leads to my house and climb it in record time with my only thought being my head hitting the pillow. When I reach the top, I stop to take a breather.

I look up.

Fuck me.

I forgot that was all there.

I couldn't look away.

The present. AVA is sitting in the same spot as she began — looking up at the stars.

So, here I am, laying on the grass patch by my house, looking up. At you. Your sky is so still. At this moment I have never felt more at peace. We're alike, me and you. I think we get each other. Especially on a night like tonight, when I've spent the majority of my evening being forgotten.

That's how you must feel, no? Abandoned by the world that lives beneath you. Because we've replaced your shining light with artificial illuminations. Just a simple switch and the city is aglow. You must be pretty scared. If we don't pay attention to you now, when you fade away will we even notice?

She whispers to the audience.

And with that, I'm acknowledged.

The stars answer my question through a strange constellation I've never seen before.

A question mark made up of stars.

She speaks again to the stars.

It's a tough question, I know.

Pause.

I've spent all evening trying to be seen.

To feel a connection.

But I suppose we have each other.

For now, anyway.

The End.

Granny, Are You a Hedgehog?

By Eva Gaynor-Smith

In memory of Elizabeth Mary Harry, a wonderful Grandmother, Mother, Sister and fierce friend. Here's to you sitting with your feet in a stream after a long walk, gazing up at the sky with a pint in hand. Cheers Granny, thank you for all the bedtime stories, here's one for you. Goodnight, God Bless.

— Your Girls x

MINNIE. Go on, have a good sniff . . . it's not what you think. No, stop it, that's dirty.

I am quite clearly talking to my dog, Bonnie.

Nope, you're not having a soggy pizza crust — don't look at me like that.

Takes a deep breath and looks up to the night sky. Speaks to her Granny.

What would you make of all this eh? Me, walking my one-eyed spaniel with PTSD and a face like a slapped arse, round the block near midnight. You'd probably tell me to put another layer on, and that my neck has enough air whistling round it you're surprised pneumonia hasn't already set in.

We voted the other week, some element of change, yet to be revealed.

I keep thinking about Bagpuss, what he would have thought of me, had he met me. Probably too loud, too short and too dramatic. But then again, he was married to you, so maybe not.

I moved to Liverpool. I know, the big leap across the M62. Hull misses me (obviously) but the hospitality and customer service industry of the North West needed this unemployed actor more than Yorkshire . . . so here we are.

I know what you're dying to say — sorry, probably shouldn't say *dying* — but why did we scatter a bit of you on a cow pat? Now, before you get those elbows out, it was Aunty Lib's idea, and I remembered to put you by the stream at Chapel Stile.

To audience.

Not long after she died, my cousin said my Granny was a
hedgehog now. This is not unusual: we are all a bit
excentric in our own right. I thought she was making an
apt observation to her sometimes-prickly attitude, but no.
She truly believed at that time my Granny had taken on a
new form as a lactose intolerant, small but gentle, and
childhood-fear-inducing protecter of road safety
awareness: a hedgehog. Shuffling in the dark, most likely
on the hunt for a packet of Rolos . . .

Can hedgehogs eat Rolos?

Gesturing to the dog. Talking to Granny.

You'd love her. She's bat shit, but she's also held us
together this last year. If you have any say up there,
could you send down some good news? I mean we'll take
anything — just not rain, please no more rain!

It's been a lot, I won't lie, but you know that. Grasping on
to moments of quiet in the chaos feels like all I have been
able to do, Granny. It's like a wave at high tide,
magnificent, crashing, destructive, plosive, wonderful
and relentless. I wish it'd slow down for a bit. Take stock
like people in retirement do, reflecting on their lives.
Their past, present and future, with that glimmer of
optimism. Do you remember it all now, by the way? Did
a button reset when you left us? Has my name returned
to you? No longer 'Minnie Mouse', but my solid, given
name, one that you held for fourteen years with a
tenderness and love of a lifetime. I'm sorry. I'm sorry you
lost so much.

The only place I can really 'see' you now is out here. Not
from Liverpool or even Hull so much, but the biggest sky
I know, cascading over the East Yorkshire coast like a
midnight blanket of memories. You are to the left of
Bagpuss, Grandad is just above, Uncle Ed far down to the

right near the Ursa Major constellation, and Phillipa is in that little cluster, because to be without a pack of women just wouldn't be right.

Wonder what Labour will do about it? Maybe they'll say they'll halve the amount of satellites currently orbiting, or maybe they'll start bringing them down with a giant spacey sky scooper. Or maybe they will just say things and not do anything. We've come to expect that from politicians, as you know. Well, I suppose it's not really us is it? It's that Elon Musk. Oh, you'd despise him.

BONNIE pulls on the lead.

Hey, come on, no street snacks today.

To audience.

My Granny had the sharpest elbows known to man. In fact, there will be a record somewhere detailing the extraordinary feats to which the pointiness of her elbows was magnified from birth, and how they became a weapon of mass destruction for anyone who tried to touch her golden syrup without asking first.

Wrestling announcer style:

In the blue corner, a small man with too much money and not enough brain cells, it's Elon Musk. And in the red corner, it's Mary 'The Elbows' Mania, fighting for the stars and solar system.

To audience.

I reckon she'd win, smack him with a *Radio Times* and then sing *All Things Bright and Beautiful* till he begged for mercy. I inherited no boniness but instead sarcasm and the unbearable desire to be near a body of water at all times, like a golden retriever. If I am away from the sea or any mass of water for too long, I distort into a sickly, sad,

Victorian child. Think Beth in *Little Women*, take me to the sea to cure me . . . well not for Beth I suppose. Spoilers.

To Granny.

Basically, you've probably already noticed, but he keeps sending these things called 'Starlink' up into space — his way of letting whatever lives up there know that he's got a massive penis, obviously. He's like those boy racers with amped up cars that rev past you as you are at a zebra crossing, trying to exert their dominance in whatever way they can.

We're told it's helping remote communities and access to healthcare, but maybe we are just *assuming* what these remote communities need instead of *asking* them? It just means that you're starting to fade. Each time I look up I'm finding it harder and harder to pinpoint exactly where you are.

I can feel you everywhere, like when I'm dipping my toes in a rocky stream or when I am nervous before an interview and I hear you say, 'Shoulders back, stand up straight and shape.' But somehow, this doesn't feel enough. I want to know you are all there, see you like a physical, prominent light emitting down to me. I want you to see back, too. To see me grow, not in height, but hopefully as a person. Make all the mistakes, sometimes repeatedly, and keep my head up high. Drag my feet along worn paths of decades gone by, chatting to the sheep, pretending they know all of the agricultural gossip. You're fading.

Bonnie, stop pulling! What is it? Come here.

Oh shit.

It's a hedgehog.

Nah, that's freaky. Did I just summon a hedgehog?

I'm putting that on my Spotlight CV straight away: can sing alto, classical, and summon hedgehogs.

To Bonnie.

Nope you're not having it, Mrs.

To audience.

It seems confused, sort of tilting in and out of the streetlight.

On a bad day memory wise, my Granny asked why two ladies were holding hands. My aunty pointed out that they were lesbians, to which she loudly replied in the middle of Mountain Warehouse, 'Dustbins! Now that's cruel, they might just like each other'.

I can't see a hedgehog shouting at anyone, so maybe she wouldn't be a hedgehog.

What do I do? Erm, hello little one, let's create a bit of darkness for you, yeah?

Pulls off coat and shades a small area away from the dog, so that the hedgehog can pass in the dark. She sits in this moment of quiet. The hedgehog shuffles off the path into the undergrowth.

Swear that hedgehog smiled at me. Can a hedgehog smile?

Chuckling to herself.

Maybe it is my Granny. Granny? Or maybe I've finally lost the plot . . . do hedgehogs have pointy elbows?

This is silly now. Come on then Bon, let's get back home.

Starts to walk away, stops and looks up.

Granny? If you are there, please don't fade. Keep showing me you're there in some way, even if you feel like being a hedgehog one day, or a robin the next, or even the brightest star shining down at me. Just let me know you're there, I still need you.

Sighs, and resumes her walk with the dog.

Come on you.

The End.

Feel the Fizz

By Eleanor Hall

A WOMAN. She holds a metal carbonated can in one hand, and a phone in the other. Throughout the piece, she does not let go of the can.

WOMAN. When I say I work night shifts cleaning offices, I don't mean the ones belonging to the estate agents above the chippy. I'm talking about the type that are stacked high in a building, a building that's . . . you know . . . shaped like a carrot high on violence or a big glass bunion. Tonight, I meet this mammoth of a skyscraper. White glass that rises viciously into the night.

My ears pop in the lift but settle once the doors open at Level 64. I am greeted by an army of double-headed monitors, conjoined techno-twins enslaved to endless rows of desks. Capitalism at its most clinical, but yet to be cleaned by me. With my cleaning apron wrapped round me ready, I'm the child of Orion and Dettol.

Becomes aware of the can in her hand.

It catches my eye, sitting alone on a desk. Their prized product, so familiar, so firmly cemented in the ancient culture of my youth. I take it in my hand and it's cool to the touch, and suddenly I'm sixteen again, witnessing my sister pour vodka in, giggling as it trickles into the fizz. On that open field, the sky's decorated with bright promises. As I wipe the screens and clean those endless rows of desks, I can hear that childish laughter. I keep an eye on the can as I change the bins. It was 49p, back then.

As I crash into bed at 6am, I feel my partner stir and roll outwards to go to work. We're in this orbital flow. I don't mind. But I can't remember the last time we met eyes, or shared snores.

Becomes aware of the phone in her hand.

3pm, and this metal buzzes for attention. A formal voice connects our call, and then my sister pounces into speech:

'Hi! It's me, you okay? How was your night at the Death Star? It's a wonder your hands aren't really dry off all that scrubbing! Are they dry? Have you tried O'Keefe's?'

She's only been in there one month, but her words have gotten faster and faster. And when I ask her why, she goes:

'I'm like, fizzing, you know! So much energy, nowhere to put it! I know people come in here and they sleep all day but I'm not doing that, nah, no way, I'm not gonna waste away snoring. Boring! Do you know how bad that fucks up your circadian rhythms? Cos if you sleep all day—'

I begin to explain that I sleep all day.

'Yeah, but you're being proactive at night, getting your daily bread and whatnot. Hey, you wanna see my arms, cos I'm doing a hundred pull-ups every day off this bunk bed. Listen, the only way is up! Eleven months and I'm out!'

I mention the news, but I'm quickly cut off by her energy—

'No, I'm not letting my brain go mushy on telly! Eh, I've nearly finished *Jane Eyre*! I'm at the bit where she goes a bit doolally, you know, hearing voices from across the hills.'

Then she lists the other books she's gasping to get through. She mentions poncy books, dusty books, books that are basically bricks of paper. I want to tell her about the news again. About what they're up to on Level 64 of the Death Star.

'I think it's the law, you know! They have to provide us with a library!'

About the stunt they're launching.

'And God, the amount of *Crime and Punishments* they've got! I wonder if having that many copies is a deliberate thing . . . '

Instead, I listen. I can't help but smile at her pull-ups and her books. Who am I to destroy the lilts of contentment in her voice? I just keep listening.

The call ends.

Eight sunrises pour through the tall glass of Level 64; my ears pop eight times over in that stupid lift. With each shift, more information sparkles and catches my eye. The more I tell myself to stop, the more I find myself searching. Eyes darting behind monitors. 'Accidentally' testing the locked drawers. I spend twenty minutes cleaning the same spot, as I stare at paper plans of past prototypes. I'm hoovering and I notice I'm sucking up little twinkles from the floor. I peer down: it's glass. Someone's smashed it and nobody's bothered to pick it up.

One afternoon before work, I pop into the corner shop by mine. The can is now four quid. Four quid? The shop keeper tells me it's in demand cos of the stunt they'll be doing, so he has to inflate the price to keep up. He says sorry, but I pass my coins over to him anyway, wondering: am I part of the problem?

More sunrises pour through the building and make my head heavy; the bursting sun claims the sky for the day. Home time. Crashing into bed at 6am, I feel my partner stir, roll outwards, go to work. An orbital flow that I don't mind. Can't remember the last time we met eyes. Can't remember the last time we met.

It's a week before the launch. I'm two hours into my shift and I come across a monitor that's been left on. The corporate branding boasts its brilliant face all over the screen; a screensaver slurring across the dark pixels.

Becomes aware of the can in her hand.

I probably shouldn't turn it on. Cos that would get me in trouble.

But I wiggle the mouse and in a flash there it is. On some software I don't recognise.

Their plans to take over the sky. Then I see emails. More software. Tabs after tabs of it. A database of power; a library of opportunity.

And then a voice comes to me across the city, penetrating the windows of Level 64 and then my chest, to communicate a very simple command:

'Delete'.

And my heart pounds as I take in all these tabs and their inviting crosses, saying 'Delete, delete.'

And before my grip can tighten on the mouse, I drop everything and leave my shift, pacing through the streets, passing drunk city revellers that shout into the heavy summer air. I steal glances from above. No moon tonight. Instead, the sky is a luminous cloud, smeared with the sodium tinge of streetlamp orange.

Back to the phone.

'You know, I've started a book club! Listen to this from Dostoyevsky. Not from *Crime and Punishment*, I didn't get great responses off that one, but in this other one he says this:

At a normal pace.

'It was a marvellous night, the sort of night one only experiences when one is young. The sky was so bright, and there were so many stars that, gazing upward, one couldn't help wondering how so many whimsical, wicked people could live under such a sky.'

I can't stop thinking about this bloody launch. I take the next shift off to try and readjust, but I'm glued to my phone for hours on end. My sleep hormones get sucked dry from hours of doomscrolling, quick clips nicking melatonin, soundbites lassoing around my focus, tightening and squeezing and my head hurts like the scream of the sun at the end of a shift. So, frothy with exhaustion and outrage, I march to the corner shop. The can's probably a fiver at this point. I walk past the shopkeeper, down the aisle, and place this —

Becomes aware of the can in her hand.

— dull, sad mirror back on the shelf.

And then: launch night. I reach the Death Star but I don't go in. Instead, I stand in the street, crane my neck and stare at the building, thinking about the hive of corporate excitement around their world-first operation. I'm an expectant face in a growing crowd, as people pool onto the street, counting down to midnight, and I think about the growing ache at the back of my head, and as I glimpse some bright thing way east of where I should be looking – the North Star? Or some planet? I dunno — I squeeze my phone as a promise to myself to email a resignation.

We're reaching two, then one, then there's a burst of clapping and whooping. Here goes.

Satellites, lavishly scattered 'cross the sky, align in a red constellation. Giant capital letters read:

FEEL THE FIZZ.

I focus my gaze on the . . . is that the . . . ?

Yeah, it is. They've used the moon as a full stop.

In that moment of realisation, I feel something bubble within me. Heavy and sickening.

A rising sensation that—

Cracks open can.

—the sentence doesn't end there.

The End.

They Call Me ALAN

By Mollie Hurrell

ALAN. They call me Alan.

I have had many shapes, many forms, many modes of being, if you will. I might be a streetlamp, or a nightlight, the LED strips strung up inside a multi-storey car park, or the heart-shaped fairy lights dangling in your back yard. I have travelled far and wide, visited every major city, every highway, every billboard, in fact there are very few places I haven't been. But my favourite place is the coast, the way the water sparkles when I'm close, casting out rays far across the ocean. I come here when I need to think, to take stock, to feel okay. And right now, I really need that.

I have always wanted to make a name for myself, to be noticed, to be a star. You name something, you acknowledge it has a purpose, you give it meaning. It's only in the past few decades that I've really been noticed in that way.

They call me ALAN. It's not a very fancy name, but I guess I like it, it's better than my full name (Artificial Light at Night) which, to be honest, is a bit of a mouthful, and a bit too formal for my liking. Makes me feel like I'm on trial, or like I'm in trouble at school or something. It's not what I would have chosen for myself. I have often wondered why I couldn't have been called Leo or Andromeda or maybe Lynx, yeah Lynx would have been cool. But no, Alan is what they came up with, it's just never really felt like it suited me. But I guess it could have been worse.

My family have been around for a while now, ever since the great race of legend, where Swan and Edison battled it out to invent the first incandescent light bulb. Back in those days, artificial light was a marvel, a miracle, people used to stop in the streets and stare at them as though they were stars fallen to Earth just for them. In April 1900, they took my great great grandpa to the Paris Exposition, where he cameoed as the Spirit of Electricity. He used to wax lyrical about the Palace of Light, where he stood holding a 50,000-volt torch aloft and illuminating the positively charged future for everyone to see. Surrounded by electrical cars, escalators and magnificent telescopes showing images of the moon and the planets, he represented the cutting edge of the new era, the stuff of hope, ingenuity and dreams. We were lightning and energy moulded, made useful. Back in those days everything crackled with potential and excitement.

My ancestors weren't just there to look pretty either, they were useful too. They lit the cities, shone down on the roads, soon there wasn't an apartment or a street that they didn't brighten up a bit. They guarded the towns as they stayed up later and later, the cars beetling along into the early hours of the morning. To hear their stories, you'd think they were warriors or something, they were so proud to have done their bit.

But that was before my time. I was born at the end of the great roll out. I wasn't made to be useful, to be a symbol of a new dawn: I was the amped-up, full-voltage version of my predecessors. I was engineered to shine everywhere, all at once, all the time. No longer satisfied with a scattering of light to illuminate a riverbank or a single lighthouse calling in the ships as pappa had done, they wanted me to be more than that, brighter, bigger, longer lasting, to light the night sky till it glowed blue-white like day. Like any kid whose dreams are picked out for them by their parents, I wanted to make them happy. I have always wanted to please people, to be loved and adored. It's just something inside me, like I'm hardwired that way. So I threw myself into it, with everything I had.

I worked like a honeybee, painting the world orange with every last drop of energy. Every street, every nighttime memory, I lacquered with amber light, till it dripped sickly sweet like honey. My great great ancestors may have been to Paris, but had they lit up the miniature Eiffel Tower in Vegas? Or chaperoned an Elvis-themed wedding whilst simultaneously screaming that there was a two-for-one sale at Barneys? I was a businessman, a gambler, and a late-night entertainer. I was a priest and a poet, an artist and conman. I held the world in an endless sunset that gave way to dawn without a breath.

I used to idolize the heavens. After all, when you're nocturnal like me, there aren't many other role models to look up to. I used to watch the zodiac wheeling above my head, to listen to the stories of the ram and the lion, the hook and the swan. I wanted people to look at me like that, to view me like they did the constellations, with wonder and awe.

So, I began to change. I got rid of the tacky orange, opting for something cleaner, more classic. I swapped out the sodium for LEDs, and my light turned bluer, cooler, like starlight. I did the work, became leaner, fitter, able to swim deeper into the oceans, to climb higher into the atmosphere — all the time a small voice in my head asked why? There was nothing for me in any of these places, no one to witness my effort, nothing to help or reveal.

I ignored that voice. This was how I was going to make it: this was gonna land me my place amongst the stars.

Soon there wasn't a cranny or nook I didn't fill with my light. But I was tired, so exhausted, and looking around I noticed that everyone else seemed to be tired too. The people stayed up later, blue light pouring from their screens which they seemed unable to put down. The birds, too, seemed to gravitate towards me. But though I was glad of the company, their presence made me sad, for when they arrived they seemed confused, their feathers ruffled, as though they weren't quite sure why they had come, like I had let them down somehow with false promises. Their disappointment unsettled me.

I was in my blue phase, and everything around me seemed stripped back, downtrodden and forlorn. Like I was stuck in an early Picasso painting unable to get out.

Then came the blame, the hate, and it was so unexpected, so out of the blue (thank you) that I nearly blacked out.

It was the astronomers first. They were pissed because they had to trek out into deep forests in order to see the stars. Fair enough, I thought, fair enough, that is their job after all. But then everyday people started to join in.

'We can't see Orion or his star-studded belt!' they cried, 'or Scorpio or the Big Dipper! And where is Aquarius, that big water-bearing bear you?!'

They turned on me, fingers pointing.

'It's Alan's fault!' they said, 'It's Alan's mess', they cried.

All I have ever wanted is to be a star. I had modelled myself on these heroes, these titans of the sky, and my makers, my so-called allies, had the gall to paint me as the villain, after the years of service I had given them!

That's when I began to break down. I refracted, splitting and bouncing off the walls, off the clouds, off the damned satellites floating up in orbit. My pain was a like a migraine, white hot and blinding. I only glowed brighter, branding the map of the world into space like a real star, and the death of it took everything I had.

I just wanted to rest. Let me rest!

I return to the sea, this place that shimmers when I draw close, that still makes me feel special. I watch the fish gather about my legs, their silky bodies circling like dogs that can't escape their own tails. Like moths gathering around me, the world swishes and spins, pressing in from every side. Everyone wants a piece of me, but no one seems to know what to say when they get it. Blank eyes, dishevelled faces, cool stares have become my reality. Is this what it feels like to be a star? To be loved from a distance, but to feel eternally alone?

How did things get this way? Days blur into days, my sense of time feels warped and wrong. If I am a star, should I not hold the secrets of seconds, the weight of years, in my hands? If I am a star, why do I feel so disconnected? It's the space between stars where the magic happens, the endless possibility for connection between each glimmering spark that has caught our attention for millions of years and will continue to do so for countless more.

But I guess we don't think about what it's like to actually be up there blazing until there's nothing left — that at the heart of every star there is a sun. It's no wonder I'm burnt out, that I can't hold it together. I need space. I need to feel part of something again, to reconnect with what I really am. I can feel it now, the darkness when the oil burns low, when the turbines stop turning and the light goes out. A star cannot live forever, nothing can. It may seem as though they have been around since the dawn of time, but the age of stars will end as all things do. And my time to shine is nearly done.

It's time to turn off the light, to flick the switch, to dim the day.

Maybe one day, if I stop wasting my time and energy on things that don't really matter, I'll stop trying to be a star — and just be me.

The End.

Olive Branch

By Martha Jamieson

Night. OLIVE takes in the surroundings of her garden. She looks proud. Something catches her attention. She tends to a plant, looking at how much it's grown. She smells it. She bends down with a slight strain to pick a weed.

Singing:

OLIVE. There's a worm at the bottom of the garden and his name is Wiggly Woo.

Addressed to the sky.

Wonder if we'll have any glow-worms tonight? They're not worms, they're beetles. The females are just fabulous, really glam actually. They emit a green and orange glow from their backsides at nighttime, climb up plant stems and gleam to attract mates.

Bit like the young girls wearing sequins in Concert Square on a Friday night.

OLIVE looks to the side and squints, her eyes strained from the light. She stands on her tiptoes looking over the fence.

Not again.

New couple has moved in next door. They're young. Hosting dinner parties nearly every night in that back garden of theirs. Think they should go into business, open a restaurant, call it Poke Bowl Illuminations. They've got fairy lights wrapped round every branch, LEDs coating every strand of grass. You can cut out the hour's drive to Blackpool to see the lights now, you just have to get an invite for tea round at theirs.

Talking of which, I got a handwritten note through my letterbox from them yesterday asking me if I'd like to go round one night this week. It said on it in scrawny writing: 'DISCLAIMER — we only cook and eat plant-based, hope this is okay!' Big exclamation mark at the end of it, and a very wonky smiley face.

Like I haven't smelled and seen their refried beans and harissa-roasted everything. I feel like shouting over the fence: 'Darling, I was vegetarian in an era of meat and two veg! The only plant-based lifestyle I experienced was malnourishment and judgement!'

I don't know their names. They didn't sign them on the note, but I've christened them 'Alan' and 'Alana'. Since they're beneficiaries of A.L.A.N — Artificial Light at Night — I'll have them labelled as that.

OLIVE turns towards the fence.

Oh, hello Alan.

Welcome to the neighbourhood.

I wasn't admiring the lights, no.

I don't mean to iterate some kind of Neighbourhood Watch rhetoric, but artificial light at night has colossal impacts, you know.

Can you hear those songbirds?

Yes?

Well songbirds sing in the morning.

And it's not the morning, is it?

It's all them lights, you see. Triggers their dawn response.

It makes their feeding and breeding all off kilter. Imagine someone wakes you up in the middle of the night, gets you all dressed and ready for work, then tucks you back into bed, only to wake you in an hour's time and take you through the whole process again.

To the audience.

If my Leo was here now. He'd be round there giving him what for.

I miss him.

I miss him most when it rains.

We used to sit in our greenhouse and listen to it tap dancing on the ceiling. Sometimes even stand outside in it and slow dance to its irregular rhythms.

It was mad, I know! Caught many a cold from doing that — but it was always worth it.

OLIVE's attention is drawn to a moth passing by.

Oh look — a clouded border moth, off to find food by the light of the moon.

More than half the world's species are nocturnal. He basically was.

We didn't have many pet names for one another, only one. I was Sun and he was my Moon.

Beat.

It wasn't all candles and roses. He'd sleep in the day whenever he could to catch up on lost kip after being up all night, looking at constellations, aurora, and the Big Dipper. I always made sure to turn in by nine o'clock. Looking back, it was resentment, some kind of punishment.

Beat.

Now I'm a night owl. Sit out in the garden till all hours looking up at the sky.

My mother told me something when I was a teenager that always stuck with me. She said grief is harder when you're grieving a relationship that didn't exist with a person.

It's more painful because you're mourning what you didn't have.

We started to drift further apart. He was up there (*looks up to the sky*), I was down here (*looks to the ground.*)

On nights where the only conversation that passed between us was 'Mmm, this is nice, thank you dear', accompanied by the scraping of cutlery, I'd think back to the night we got married.

We celebrated, just the two of us, sitting barefoot in the park talking, drinking, and eating cake, lit by the stars.

My bare feet were glued to the ground, his neck strained looking up to the sky. Me the nature conservationist, him the astronomer.

We talked a lot about life and death that night.

Romantic I know.

Had a celebrant who really got into the till death do you part bit. Think that's what sparked it.

Leo said if there's an afterlife and if you got to choose your form, he'd quite fancy being a star. Less responsibility than being my Moon!

I sometimes pretend he's playing hide and seek with me. Gliding around as a star, forming new shapes, joining new constellations.

I play dot-to-dot with the stars, just in case I spot one that reminds me of him.

OLIVE's tone shifts from soft and reflective to accusatory.

To ALAN.

What did you just say to me?

Why do I care so much about your outdoor lighting?

You what?

How's it affecting me?

Soon, I won't be able to see him any more. The sky will be too bright for me to spot him.

Don't you get it? He's a star in the sky, and because of you I'm as far away from him as I was when he was alive.

There's things I never got to say to him.

I just want to feel close to him and you're stopping it! You're blocking it. People like you just couldn't begin to understand. It's self-indulgent. Give me one reason, one reason why you need that many lights on.

Beat. Cynically.

Your little girl is frightened of the dark.

She might be frightened of the dark, mate, but she'll be more frightened when there's no stars left in the sky.

Beat. OLIVE's face falls.

She *was* frightened of the dark. The lights are for her.

Beat.

I — I'm so sorry.

I get it now.

Beat.

Tell me about her.

OLIVE intently listens and nods, holding her gaze for several beats.

No parent should ever have to bury their child.

Beat.

You feel her presence in those lights, don't you?

Are the pink windmills for her too?

They move beautifully.

Beat.

They dance how she did?

Rosie?

She was a ballerina?

Beat.

I learned that when small stars die they slowly cool. They continue to glow after they die.

It sounds like she still glows so brightly.

I think my Leo has carried on glowing. I get *glimpses* of him in nature — but *always* in the stars.

Beat.

We've had quite the first encounter, haven't we?

OLIVE gently laughs.

It's a good mantra to have, that. 'Life is too short for small talk'. I'll use that.

Thank you for sharing your story with me.

I didn't catch your name.

Francis?

I'm Olive.

Why did I call you Alan before? Sorry, I just thought you looked like one.

Beat.

You going in?

Night night love. I'll look out for you out here.

We sit with OLIVE for a beat as she processes the encounter with FRANCIS.

I think on Earth we formulate our own mini planets. We find our satellites, we become their orbits. Maybe we're on the surface of one another's planets now, me and him next door.

OLIVE looks down to her watch before looking up at the sky

It's time to say goodnight to my Moon.

We hear music. OLIVE begins to sway. Her movements are soft and gentle. Her arms are out, as if wrapped around the shoulders of another. She simulates a soft slow dance just as her and Leo did in the rain.

The End.

My Lost Spark

By Ellie Sammer

LUNA. I often wonder what it's like to be you. I'm not jealous but I've seen the way she sparkles for you, and you don't even see her. I'm hopelessly in love with Celeste, an eternal being scattered across the heavens. An intangible light, she'll never exist in my gaze, yet you can bask in her glory each night whilst my ever-slight atmosphere longs for her presence. In another universe I know she would have been mine, but here we are living in parallel, lost love this time.

Earth, I am trapped in your orbit, always facing you, always crossing paths, but always surrendering to your dominance. She used to inspire you, guide your people and be admired for her vastness. You named her, wove stories around her, made flags and patterns of her. You named her constellations, saw heroes and gods in her, and she is the muse of all your astronomers. Celeste was your guide, your compass in the dark. Earth, why would you ignore her?

Now, your people, now they seek a brighter light, a light they can manipulate, one that between you and me is doing more harm to you than me. They are blinded by the artificial lights they have created. These lights, these fleeting glimmers of human discovery, have drawn their attention away from the eternal splendour of Celeste. Their future is losing sight of the natural wonder that once captivated their souls.

Celeste's light will forever be eternal, even if you lose sight of her. She's a timeless wonder, whilst your artificial light will only ever be temporary. You can build bigger and brighter, but nothing will be more intense than the woman you had and chose to ignore. She's not someone you can pick up and drop off — when she's out of sight she'll be gone forever. I'm aware of the animals you've loved and lost on Earth and I didn't think you'd be capable of this in our space.

Your people once worshipped Celeste and I: we were the celebrities of the sky, and light and darkness were the symbols of good and evil. They loved the mystery of how we carried a bridge between earthly and divine realms — secrets we held from you because we know what power has done to you. The Sun has whispered to me about your people fighting for what is right — this gives me hope — but there shouldn't be a fight at all, especially not about the night.

Your oceans are crying, their seabeds are dying, and the corals can't carry on. Earth, why can't you see? You know what you're missing, but you'll never listen. The humans, they see themselves differently from Celeste and I, but they too are made from stardust, they just can't see you — only sometimes in the sparkle in their lover's eye.

Earth, you have my Celeste under lock and key, but with each passing night she slips further away. To love is to lose and you are losing. I've tried warning you but my relationship with the waves can only do so much, and I too am drifting away from you. Without her, your nights lose their magic and their soul. When there's nothing to wish upon, no one can make your dreams come true. Who will be the protagonist in all of those dreams?

Earth, I'm reaching out from afar, hoping you'll take a moment to truly appreciate the incredible beauty of Celeste in the sky. Her light is fleeting, and you never know when it might be gone for good. I've watched you change and seen how you've been hurt, and I fear the same fate might befall her. Look up and let Celeste's light bring wonder back to your nights and fill your heart with awe. For without her, the tapestry of your night sky unravels, and the magic that once was will fade into the shadows of what could have been. But it's not too late, Earth. Lift up your gaze and renew your bond with the celestial wonder above. As I orbit endlessly, I will hold onto the hope that you will once again see the lost spark in her light.

Good night.

The End.

Astra's Last Livestream

By Angelica Willis

A tired middle-aged woman walks to the stage and sets up her mirror, phone and tripod on a table. She looks at her reflection in her mirror and sighs in annoyance. She rolls her eyes then taps the screen on her phone and puts on a fake smile.

ASTRA. Wow hello everyone on the Internet . . . This is all new to me so bear with me. I thought I would do my skin care with you and talk about my new song coming out very soon.

ASTRA grabs her bag from the floor. She speaks as she takes out various skincare items. She looks at her phone with an amazed expression.

I guess this skin care thing is a trend with you guys. Wow, I cannot believe I have 500 of you watching me. That is amazing. Also, I can see your messages too, how lovely.

ASTRA places a script on the table in a spot that her online audience is not able to see. She holds up a serum and shows the audience. She begins to apply the serum and glances over at the script as she speaks.

I am using this. It is a wrinkle-free retinol serum from the Starry Starry Night skincare range. I have been applying this for years and until I find a better one I am not changing my skincare routine. You can use my promo code ASTRA20 for a 20 per cent discount. Remember to check out all the products by Starry Starry Night — they have all your skincare needs, like serums, moisturisers . . .

ASTRA tries to covertly flip the page of her brand sponsorship script.

And they sell eye creams and face masks too. Their products are just amazing for the skin.

ASTRA sings as she applies her serum.

Am I wishing on a star or a satellite for you to be my love tonight?

ASTRA pauses to read the comments on her phone. She swipes her finger along the screen as she speaks.

Yes, that is a lyric from my new song *Satellite*, which features the hip-hop star Spacejunk. He also produced the song. It is a bit of a different sound than what I have put out . . . but I know you'll all love it.

ASTRA pauses for a moment and tries to figure out what to do next. She scrambles in her bag to find her next product.

Umm, sorry guys, I'm just trying to find — yes, this product which is . . .

ASTRA reads the label.

Moon Pebbles Pimple Cream. I am putting this on now to hide all of this.

ASTRA gestures to the marks on her face and smiles. She struggles to open the packaging of the pimple cream as she talks.

When I had some time away from the public eye, my skin was the clearest and brightest it had ever been. It was so shiny — not oily, by the way. But now I am back in the city and it has not been great. Far back, you probably can't see it, but if you guys were here in person and up close you could see all my blemishes.

ASTRA notices that her viewer count has lowered since she first began the live stream. She takes a deep breath and hides her frustration with a laugh.

My viewer count has dropped by 250 . . . is that a glitch? What does L in the chat mean?

ASTRA starts to apply the pimple cream on some spots on her face. She hides her discomfort and irritation with a smile. Whispers.

Ah, this stings.

ASTRA rubs the cream quickly with a fake smile. She notices a username that captures her attention.

Oh, hello astrologygirlie, it has been a while since I've last seen you. I guess it's because I haven't been touring. Those flowers you gave me at my last show were beautiful . . . how are you — why don't you like my music anymore? What do you mean I am washed up and irrelevant? I thought you were my fan . . .

ASTRA closes her eyes and looks away from the camera to hide her expression. She bites her lip to try not to cry. When she opens her eyes, she frowns and clenches her fist.

You know what? I am tired of trying to be entertaining by doing brand deals that cause more harm than good. I am going to be real. I am sick of the music industry upholding and pushing these types of so-called 'pop stars' into the scene. They are fake. They are manufactured. I had to work hard with no team and no money when I first started. These guys have everything handed to them. I've seen these so-called new 'pop stars' on big and bright billboards all over the city when it should be me up there. They don't know that the music industry is everchanging. You could be selling out shows and performing at large arenas then the next minute the music industry can remove you and you are gone. Invisible and vanished from everyone . . .

Now my viewer count is less than 100 — you guys would rather me sell you all these meaningless products? I am being honest and now you're leaving.

ASTRA closes her eyes to calm herself down. She reminisces on a memory of when she was a young performer.

I remember performing at my first show. I had stage fright, and I was nervous, but I saw everyone's faces beaming with large smiles. Smiles that lit up the whole venue. I felt a rush like no other. Just seeing everyone cheering and chanting my name gave me the confidence and energy to go out there and shine. You guys singing and dancing along to every song. I thought the cheering was loud when I first came on stage but the sound of roars for an encore was crazy. I just had to go back out there and perform again. That was the first time I felt alive and I felt like a true star. You guys loved me. But as time went by, I slowly faded more and more into the abyss, and other pop stars who were inspired by me got more credit and recognition. I wonder what happened . . . did my songs sound too different to what everyone else was creating? Could you guys sense that I was burnt out from performing due to my music becoming less and less popular? Did you lose interest as I got older?

ASTRA takes a deep breath to calm herself down.

I guess there are only 50 of you watching now. I am sorry about my rant . . . I was meant to talk about my new song . . . my label said that if it does not chart, they will terminate my contract . . . I just ended up ranting about pop stars . . . maybe this is not the best way to promote my music. Who am I kidding? Doing TikTok livestreams? This isn't me. To be honest, I don't even care about the new song and maybe you guys can feel that. It is not me, they want me to sound like all the autotuned artificial pop on the radio.

You don't know this but the reason why I have not been in the spotlight is because I have been living in the woods and I wrote an album. My management said it would not sell but maybe if I play a song I can prove them wrong . . . the album is called *Astraphel in the Skyglow*. Astraphel means 'a lover of stars' — because I wrote this album literally under the stars.

I was spending more time in nature. There were no lights. No WiFi. Nothing. I spent most of my days writing songs and meditating. It was so peaceful and quiet . . . But at the same time, it wasn't the best experience because I love performing and I do want to be seen by you guys. I just feel like you guys don't want to see me.

ASTRA puts her phone back on the table. She grabs a guitar from underneath her and faces the audience. She begins to strum and sing.

And in the darkness, I glow

Wherever you go

But you can't feel me

I want to be light

And shine for the night

But there's no energy

You'd rather be blind

Invisible to your eye

But I am shimmering infinity

After singing, ASTRA is beaming with a smile. She turns to her phone and her smile fades.

Only one viewer . . . They were right. No one cares about my music any more. I guess that's it, then. The end of my career.

ASTRA grabs her phone in an attempt to end her livestream, but a comment catches her off guard. The comment makes her feel at ease.

'Your music is meaningful and has gotten me through difficult times. When I am sad, listening to your music gives me hope and it guides me. Please keep shining bright.'

Thank you for that . . .

Please, if you are listening, I just love being up there, performing for you. Please talk about me. Talk about my music. I don't want to disappear away.

The End.

Royal Treatment

A poem by Olivia Furness

Inspired by the fact that many creatures – such as the Spotted Ratfish – are designed to function in low light, and may be easily blinded, or worse.

Royal Treatment

They put up a tough front,
And are a delightful fright,
Venomous spine,
A few of its kind,
Rare ratfishes,

They are fearless,
They are spineless,
They are ruthless,

We are fragile,
We are delicate,
We are precious,

They act all cool,
And put up a good fight,
Like nothing can stop them,
But that isn't right,
And it doesn't make,
Harming them alright.

OTHER TITLES FROM THEATRE IN THE ROUGH

*

WILD WORDS:
An Anthology of Cross-Species Ecopoetry

In this anthology, young writers from across the UK have collaborated with elements of nature to co-author poems that seek to fuse human and non-human perspectives. Whether penned with rustling leaves, birdsong, rainfall, or the moon, these works invite you to share in the collective voice of the entire planet . . . and beyond.

ISBN: 9781-1-7393825-3-7

*

GROUND:
A Meditation on Eco-Anxiety

An anthology of creative connections between unlikely friends: the human and non-human worlds. In collaboration with their local environments, writers and artists explore the phenomenon of climate anxiety as a natural response to the ecological challenges we face.

ISBN: 978-1-7393825-1-3

Printed in Great Britain
by Amazon

45687365R00057